C

FLAGS

Theodore Rowland-Entwistle

The Brookwright Press
New York · 1988

What are Flags?

Flags are pieces of fabric attached at one edge to a mast or staff, the rest being free to fly in the wind. But they are much more important than this simple description suggests, for they carry designs that have meaning and represent their owners. A flag is a symbol of pride. Every country has its own national flag, and so do many organizations.

Symbols of pride: a guard of honor outside the Capitol Building in Washington, D.C., displays the Stars and Stripes and also the flags of the U.S. Army, Marines, Navy, Air Force and Coast Guard.

Flags have been in use for at least 3,000 years. In times of war many people have fought and died to protect their country's flag from disgrace. In the days when armies met in close contact on the battlefield, flags were used as rallying points, easily seen above the heads of the soldiers. It was considered a great triumph to capture the opposing army's flag.

Flags in war: two armies in the Middle Ages fly their banners as they prepare for battle.

5

Flags of many countries fly together at the Kenyatta Conference Center in Kenya. Care is taken that each flag is flown at the same height as all the others.

Hauling down the flag shows surrender, and the flag of a victor is flown above that of the vanquished.

Because flags have this symbolic meaning, great care must be taken when two or more national flags are flown together. In the United States, a 1942 law rules that with other flags on the same **halyard**, the U.S. flag is on top.

Many different names have been used for flags, such as **banner**, **burgee**, **colors**, **guidon, jack**, **pennon** or **pennant**, and **standard**. Most of these terms refer to the flag's shape or use. The meanings of these words have varied confusingly throughout history, but their modern meanings are given on page 30.

A flag is flown from an upright **flagpole** or flagstaff. It is attached at one edge to a rope, which is called the halyard. This rope can be raised and lowered to the required height. The vertical length of a flag

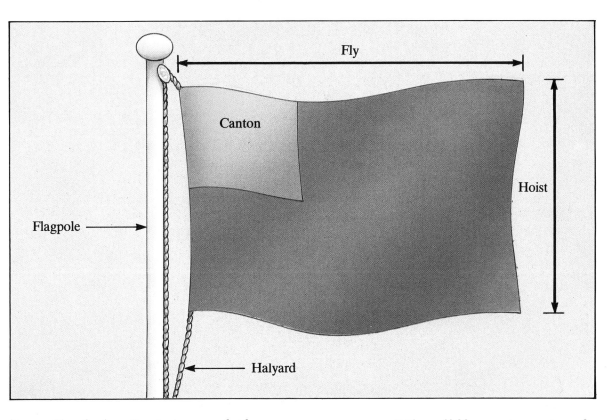

The different parts of a flag are shown here.

is called the **hoist**, and the horizontal length is the **fly**. The **canton** is the upper left-hand corner of the flag, which is next to the flagpole. Most, but not all, flags are rectangular. A flag that is triangular or tapered is called a pennant.

The study of flags is known as vexillology. This name comes from the vexillum, a banner carried by Roman soldiers.

Symbols of National Pride

The design of each country's flag has a special meaning and history. For example, the Stars and Stripes, the United States flag (also nicknamed Old Glory or the Star-Spangled Banner) has thirteen red and white stripes, symbolizing the original thirteen states, and fifty stars, one for each state belonging to the Union today. This is the latest of many U.S. flags, the first dating back to 1775 when the American colonies finally broke away from British rule.

The British Union Flag (now usually called the Union Jack) combines the ancient flags of England (the Cross of St. George), Scotland (St. Andrew's Cross) and Ireland's Cross of St. Patrick.

The Union Flag came into being in 1801 when Ireland was united

Flags are flown at times of celebration. Here the Stars and Stripes waves amid fireworks as Americans celebrate Independence Day, the Fourth of July.

with England and Scotland. The broad white band of St. Andrew's Cross should be above the red band of St. Patrick's Cross in the top left-hand corner (the canton), as shown in the picture.

The Dannebrog, the national flag of Denmark, has been in use ever since the Battle of Lyndanisse in 1219. It shows a white cross on a red background, and according to legend, it fell from heaven during the battle.

Austria's white and red flag also has its origin in war. Duke Leopold V of Austria wore a white coat over his armor during a battle in the Fifth Crusade in 1191. The cloak

The Dannebrog, Denmark's national flag, flying outside a shop in the old town of Odense.

became stained with blood, except where it was protected by his broad belt.

France's **tricolor** (a flag with three colors) dates from the French Revolution of 1789. It combines the red and blue colors of the uniforms of the Paris revolutionaries with white, the color of the uniforms of the Bourbon kings against whom they were rebelling.

The French tricolor commemorates the French Revolution of 1789. To the people of France it symbolizes liberty.

The Russian Revolution of 1917 is symbolized by the red flag of the Soviet Union, seen here at Moscow Airport.

The flag of the U.S.S.R. is red, the color that symbolizes **communism**. On it are the yellow emblems of a **hammer and sickle**, representing the struggle of the industrial and agricultural workers, which came to a head during the Russian Revolution of 1917.

Famous Flags in History

The Chinese were using flags more than 3,000 years ago. The first picture of a flag in Europe was found on a tomb built in about 400 B.C. at Paestum, a Greek colony in Italy, near Pompeii. From 100 B.C. to around A.D. 800 the only flags in regular use in Europe were the Roman vexilla, carried by Roman soldiers. It hung down from a crosspiece on a pole, as do many Church banners today. In A.D. 878 the Vikings introduced a triangular flag with a raven emblem on it.

The Bayeux Tapestry, a long piece of embroidery recording the Norman conquest of England in 1066, shows that William the Conqueror and the Normans had a **gonfanon**, a war flag with three tails, decorated with a cross. Their

Banners like these were displayed in the Middle Ages whenever knights gathered to hold a tournament. This modern version of a medieval tournament was held at Bruges, Belgium.

13

This reenactment of the Battle of Hastings in 1066 shows how the warriors of William the Conqueror carried their banners into combat.

opponents, the Saxons, led by King Harold, fought under a banner with a dragon on it. In 1195 King Richard I of England adopted the three lions that still form part of the Royal Standard.

For about five hundred years the French carried into battle a red banner with a number of tails. It was called the oriflamme. The fleur-de-lis, or lily, appeared on French flags from 1191 until the French Revolution in 1789.

Viking, Spanish, French, British, Dutch and Russian flags have all flown in North America at various times as Europeans tried to conquer the land.

When the United States declared its independence from Britain in 1776, it used a flag of thirteen stripes, with the British Union Jack in the canton. The stars in the canton, representing the states of the Union, came later. The number of stars has changed twenty-seven times as new states have joined. The present flag, with fifty stars, dates from 1960, when Hawaii became the fiftieth state.

Two American states, Georgia and Mississippi, include in their flags the old thirteen-star **Confederate** flag used by the rebel southern states in the American Civil War of 1861–5.

This is how the first flag of the United States of America looked, with thirteen stars in a ring and thirteen stripes.

The lion flag of Venice flies outside the Cathedral of St. Mark, just as it used to when Venice was an independent city-state and the cathedral was first built.

Italy's tricolor of green, white and red was first used in 1796, but did not become a national flag until 1861, when all the states that occupied Italy came together as one nation. Italy has a rich flag history from earlier years, including some famous flags such as the lion of Venice and the dragon of Naples.

Flags in Service

Flags are used for many purposes. For example, **embassies** in foreign countries identify themselves by hanging the national flag outside the building. In Britain and Canada the national flag flies over the Houses of Parliament on days when Parliament is sitting. In the United States the national flag flies over the Capital (where Congress meets) every day, whether Congress is in session or not. National flags are flown to celebrate special occasions, such as national days, victories in battle, royal weddings and anniversaries.

Canada's maple leaf flag flies on the Peace Tower of the Parliament Building in Ottawa to show that Parliament is in session.

A flag can also indicate mourning. For this it is flown at half-mast, that is, halfway up the flagpole. If an important public figure or a member of the military services dies, the coffin is draped with the person's national flag at the funeral.

In emergencies, a national flag is flown upside down as a distress signal. In wartime, a white flag, often called a **flag of truce**, is used to indicate that one side wishes to make terms or surrender.

The former royal flag of Rumania drapes the coffin of one of its kings. Flags are often used in this way, especially at state and military funerals.

Because flags were used as rallying points in battle, it is still the custom in many armies for regiments and other units to have their own flags, known as colors. In Britain a ceremony known as "trooping the color" takes place every June, in London. During the ceremony, a regimental color is trooped (paraded) in front of the monarch.

Part of the ceremony of "trooping the color," which is held every year on Horse Guards Parade in London.

Flag Language

Flags can be used to send messages, especially at sea. This was vitally important in the days before radio contact was possible between ships. The simplest form of message is the flag, or **ensign**, which a ship flies to show its nationality. This may be the same as the country's flag, but many countries have special flags for their ships.

A hoist of signal flags on an old sailing ship at a Danish carnival. Before the days of radio, such flags were the only way of sending messages from ship to ship.

Signal flags are still flown on ceremonial occasions on modern warships, as here aboard a Soviet naval ship.

When ships meet each other it is customary for them to lower their flags to half-mast and raise them again as a form of greeting. This is called "dipping." But when a warship surrenders in battle it hauls its flag down to the bottom of the mast.

Quite often a shipowner registers a ship in a foreign country to avoid heavy taxes or strict labor laws in its own country. The ship then flies the flag of this foreign country, which is known as a **flag of convenience**. To get navy protection, a ship may re-flag by re-registering in a new country. Most shipping companies have private flags, which are flown with

The national flag flies over a Mississippi paddle steamer, the "Natchez," in the harbor in New Orleans. Other flags on the ship include those of the owners.

the country's merchant navy flags. Yacht clubs also have their own flags.

Pirates used to fly a black flag with a white skull and crossbones on it, called the Jolly Roger.

Ships also use flags for signaling. There is an international set of flags with a different design for each letter of the alphabet, and pennants for the numerals. Every word can be spelled out letter by letter, but signalers also use a code in which two or three flags stand for complete words or sentences. For example, the blue and white flag for P – known as the Blue Peter – is hoisted when a ship is about to sail, and the yellow Q (for **quarantine**) flag flies if there is someone suffering from an infectious disease on board.

The flag most feared at sea was the "Jolly Roger," the skull and crossbones emblem of pirates during the 1600s and 1700s. This picture shows a "Jolly Roger" flying as a part of the fun at a fishermen's carnival.

Personal and Special Flags

It is not only nations that have their own flags. Some individuals have their own personal flags, too. This custom dates from the time when lords and knights led their people into battle, with their own banners flying. The banner carrier was a proud post, often held by a squire – a young man who hoped to become a knight.

A flag with the three fleurs-de-lis of the medieval French kings is just one of several banners showing which groups of warriors were fighting. This battle took place in Flanders in 1381.

There are still many personal flags in use today. Heads of state have them. For example, the president of the United States has his own flag, and so do the vice president and other members of the government.

A special flag: a soldier of the French Foreign Legion proudly carries the banner presented to them for heroism during World War I (1914–18).

In the coronation procession of England's Edward VI in 1547 the Royal Standard carried before him displays the French fleurs-de-lis as well as the lions of England. At that time the English kings still claimed the throne of France.

In Britain, the queen's flag is the Royal Standard. It flies over any building or ship in which she happens to be. The Royal Standard combines the ancient **coats of arms** of England and Scotland, plus the Irish harp for Northern Ireland. The Royal Standard has remained unchanged since 1837, but there were many changes before that. At one time it even included the French lily-shaped design known as the fleur-de-lis, because the English kings claimed the throne of France.

Because the Royal Standard is a British flag, the queen uses another personal standard as head of the Commonwealth, and she has different personal standards for use in Australia, Canada and New Zealand.

The first international flag was that of the Red Cross, an organization founded to help the victims of war and disaster. As it was founded in Switzerland, the Red Cross adopted the Swiss flag, a white cross on a red background, but with the colors reversed. Because the cross is a Christian symbol, the organization uses different symbols in non-Christian countries, including a red crescent in Islamic lands, a red Star of David in Israel, and a red crescent in the U.S.S.R.

Special flags are also used by international bodies such as the United Nations, the Council of Europe and the Arab League. The

Help for victims of war and disaster is symbolized by the flag of the International Red Cross. Here it is seen flying over the organization's headquarters at Geneva in Switzerland.

Some religious flags have another special meaning. These flags, outside a Buddhist shrine in Katmandu, Nepal, are prayer flags, symbolizing the hopes of the people who are flying them.

Olympic Games have had their own flag since 1913. Boy Scouts and Girl Scouts also have international flags.

Many organizations have their own special flags. Some churches have their own flags. So do religions such as the Buddhists and the Salvation Army.

Many businesses, clubs, schools and airlines now have their own flags, too. In Switzerland, every town and even tiny villages have their own flags. There is even a flag for the international association of vexillologists – those who study flags!

Special ceremonies have always been associated with flags. In the Turkish town of Marmaris the people still follow the ancient custom of flag-throwing, whirling their flags in an elaborate ritual.

Index